DIGITAL AND INFORMATION LITERACY ™

PUBLISHING YOUR E-BOOK

DANIEL E. HARMON

rosen publishing's
rosen central®

New York

Published in 2014 by The Rosen Publishing Group, Inc.
29 East 21st Street, New York, NY 10010

Copyright © 2014 by The Rosen Publishing Group, Inc.

First Edition

Library of Congress Cataloging-in-Publication Data

Harmon, Daniel E.
Publishing your e-book/Daniel E. Harmon. — 1st ed. — New York: Rosen, c2014
      p. cm. — (Digital and information literacy)
Includes bibliographical references and index.
ISBN 978-1-4488-9513-7 (Library binding)
1. Publishers and publishing—Vocational guidance—Juvenile literature. 2. Self-publishing—Juvenile literature. 3. Electronic publishing—Juvenile literature. 4. Self-publishing. I. Title.
Z286.E43 .H37 2014

070.5797

Manufactured in the United States of America

CPSIA Compliance Information: Batch #S13YA: For further information, contact Rosen Publishing, New York, New York, at 1-800-237-9932.

CONTENTS

| | | Introduction | Is There a Book Inside You? | 4 |
Introduction   4

Chapter 1   Is There a Book Inside You?   7

Chapter 2   Putting It Together   14

Chapter 3   Launching the E-Book   21

Chapter 4   Finding a Readership   28

Chapter 5   Legal Concerns and Pitfalls   34

Glossary   39

For More Information   40

For Further Reading   43

Bibliography   44

Index   46

INTRODUCTION

Even while you are young, you can become a published electronic book (e-book) author. If you have completed the draft of a book, you may be just days from launching (publishing) it in one or more e-book formats. You do not have to spend weeks, months, or years trying to find a publisher or a literary agent to represent you.

But hold on. E-book publishing is a venture not to be undertaken hastily. Think carefully about your purpose. Is your book good enough to submit to the reading public (and critics)? Put yourself in the place of readers. Will it be worth their time to read what you've written?

If you honestly can answer yes, e-publishing can be a rewarding adventure. But you have serious work to do. You must spend time preparing your e-book properly for electronic reading platforms. You should present it as attractively as you can.

Some publishing professionals believe this is the best time in history for people who love to read books—and for people who want to become authors. They point to the growing worldwide library of electronic books.

E-books have become popular for two major reasons. First, they are inexpensive. A reader can quickly download and build an impressive personal library of book files for little or no cost. Most literary classics have been converted to e-book formats. They are distributed free by resources

A tourist relaxes on a beach with an electronic reading device and a downloaded e-book. Book lovers today can carry vast libraries with them wherever they go.

such as Project Gutenberg. At the same time, thousands of new books on countless topics are free or cost very little.

Second, e-books are convenient. It's quick and easy to download them from the Internet to a computer or handheld gadget. Dozens of e-books can be contained on a pocket-size computer, dedicated reading device, or phone. They can be read wherever you are and whenever you have time.

In addition, e-books can be shared online. Thousands of e-books are available to "check out" of libraries and online services—free, for a limited period. They include best sellers and new books on timely subjects.

In the early years of e-book publishing, few popular printed books were available as e-books. Today, readers find more and more titles in both printed and e-book formats. In fact, hundreds of new books are published every day *only* in electronic formats. Readers can locate and download them almost instantly from home computers and mobile devices. If not free, e-book versions of books invariably cost less than print editions.

Writers are drawn to e-book publishing for several reasons. E-books are fairly easy to prepare and launch. Production costs are low—or free. Publication takes relatively little time, once the book is written.

E-book authors include children and teens. Some have interesting information and experiences to share. Others have a gift for writing novels, short stories, or poems.

The eventual impact of electronic publishing is unclear. Virtually all publishing professionals agree, though, that e-publishing is here to stay. That is encouraging for young writers. Breaking into print is difficult even for talented adults. Few young people find print publishers, unless they are willing to pay a vanity printing company. With e-book technology, they can publish their books themselves.

Chapter 1

Is There a Book Inside You?

Amanda Hocking began imagining stories before she entered grade school, according to reporter Ed Pilkington for the *Guardian*. A child of a broken home, she lost her troubles in reading books and writing tales of her own. By junior high school, she'd decided writing was her calling. By high school graduation, she had written dozens of stories and dabbled in novel writing.

But she couldn't get any of her work published. Time after time, her submissions to publishers were rejected. She accumulated a shoebox full of rejection notes.

In early 2010, at age twenty-six, she was working for low pay as a home care aide. She had continued to write in her off time. By then, she had completed seventeen novels in the fantasy romance genre. Mainstream book publishers had rejected all of them. One day, desperate to raise $300, she decided to publish one of her novels online as an e-book.

Hocking had few expectations. Astonishingly, she made e-book publishing history. As described by Pilkington, her vampire novel *My Blood Approves* was soon selling dozens of copies each day. Encouraged, she launched other books. Three months later, she was selling four thousand copies of her books monthly. A year later, sales were topping one hundred thousand a month.

Groundbreaking e-book author/publisher Amanda Hocking enjoys writing on her laptop computer in a coffee shop. Her spiraling self-published e-book sales led to a major book publishing contract.

Amanda Hocking soon became a millionaire author. She did it via the "indie" (independent) e-book route. Within two years, a major print publisher signed her to a high-paying contract.

Tens of thousands of talented young writers are wondering, "If Amanda Hocking could accomplish that, can't I attain at least a fraction of her success?" Most encounter frustration. But Hocking's success story demonstrates that it can be done. The world of electronic book publishing is exciting. For a young writer, it is worth exploring.

File   Edit   View   Favorites   Tools   Help

YOUNG WRITERS BECOME PUBLISHERS

YOUNG WRITERS BECOME PUBLISHERS

Ben Heckmann, an eighth-grade student in Farmington, Minnesota, was only fourteen years old when he published his second book. *Velvet Black 2* was a sequel to his first novel about the adventures of a garage band. Ben's print books are published by KidPub Press, which specializes in publishing (for a fee) books by children.

Child authors are publishing books in many categories: adventure, fantasy, horror, humor, inspirational, mystery, poetry, romance, science fiction, and sports. Some publish through companies like KidPub Press. Others prefer to publish their books themselves.

Writers always have longed to see their books in print. In the electronic book publishing age, paper books have become less necessary. Some people regard printed books ("tree-books") as environmentally harmful.

For young writers, the best thing about e-book publishing is that it is fairly simple to do. The costs are slight—or altogether free.

An Explosive Book Market

E-books generate more sales dollars than hardback books. (Softcover book sales still beat them both.) Year by year, the volume of e-book sales multiplies.

Most e-books are self-published by their writers. In Dan Poynter's *Self-Publishing Manual, Vol. 2*, the author explains that self-publishing is especially promising for writers of nonfiction books. "When you control the writing, manufacturing, distributing, and promoting, you can move faster. You can take advantage of new ideas, breaking news, changes in the book category, and changes in the audience."

Young authors are publishing e-books on countless topics. Some of the most popular are books of tips and suggestions about subjects the authors understand personally. How-to topics range from skateboarding tricks to playing a musical instrument and starting a band. Teenagers write about their experiences working or volunteering part-time. Some have written books on ethnic cooking and sports. Teen writers are also e-publishing volumes of their poetry and short stories—even complete novels.

Step One: Be Sure You Have Something to Say

The length of a book is hardly a factor in e-publishing. Most adult-level printed books contain at least eighty thousand words. Some e-books, by

Employees at a major bookstore chain examine a new e-book cover. E-book sales now exceed sales of hardbound print books, although paperbacks remain more popular.

contrast, consist of only a few thousand words. Fiction writers have published single short stories in e-book formats. An informational, magazine-style article can also be turned into an e-book. So can a handful of poems.

Credibility becomes an issue, though. Book readers expect even an e-book to be book-length—especially if it has a price tag. You could hastily format and launch a three-page school writing assignment as an e-book. However, it would be dishonest to call yourself a "published author." Unless you have real writing talent and interesting, substantial material, readers will not take your writing seriously.

The Future of Book Publishing?

Some publishing analysts suggest that electronic publishing is the future of literature. They predict "tree-books" and bookstores are doomed. Within a few years, they believe, most new books will be self-published by the authors in e-book format. Marketing and sales will be conducted almost entirely online.

This prospect disturbs critics of self-publishing. Now that almost anyone on the planet can become

Jeff Bezos, the CEO of Amazon.com, describes a new model of the company's line of electronic readers. E-reading devices are among the hottest technology gadgets in retail stores.

published, where does that leave readers? How can e-book shoppers begin to know which books are worth buying and spending time reading, and which are garbage?

Before you publish, you should ask yourself similar questions about your own book. If you publish an e-book that's sure to go nowhere, you're adding to the e-book market clutter. Your reputation as a writer may suffer.

Young authors should consider very carefully the reason to publish an e-book. If becoming wealthy and famous is your objective, you almost certainly will fail. It is much more important to consider what you have to contribute to society.

MYTHS&FACTS

MYTH E-book publishing is an easy, sure way for a young writer to achieve success.

FACT Some young authors have sold hundreds and even thousands of copies of their e-books. A few have become wealthy. The great majority, though, find fame and fortune elusive. Many sell no books at all, or only one or two per month. They often resort to giving their books to friends and relatives.

MYTH Using Internet search engines, readers interested in your book's subject will eventually locate your book.

FACT Keyword searches can find your book, but it likely will be lost among thousands of search results. No matter how good your book is, you need to develop an effective marketing plan to attract readers.

MYTH Major publishers scour the Internet looking for promising e-books by new authors.

FACT New authors are rarely discovered this way. Major publishing companies are overwhelmed with book proposals. Their acquisition staffs are kept busy evaluating submissions from literary agents and established authors.

Chapter 2

Putting It Together

Some authors—especially computer-smart young people —delight in e-book preparation. Others have no interest in formatting text, working with visual elements, or learning the technical requirements of an online publishing platform. If you have no patience for assembling the project and perfecting it so that everything looks just right, you will need to hire or recruit technical assistance.

Preparing Text

E-publishing engines are automated systems that turn the text of your book into an e-book. The text is formatted to appear attractively on the screen of a particular reading device.

Before you enter your manuscript into an e-publishing system, be sure it is "clean." Typos and misspellings will not be corrected for you; they will appear in your published e-book. Popular word processing programs have built-in spelling and grammar checkers. Still, you need to edit and proofread your work carefully. A language teacher may be willing to edit your book, or

Before you present your book for processing by an e-publishing engine, you have much work to do. Every proofreading of the document will likely expose mistakes missed earlier.

at least make suggestions. You should engage as many proofreaders as possible to look for mistakes. You yourself should read through the text repeatedly. Each time you read it, you almost certainly will find mistakes you missed or wording you want to change.

A major advantage of e-books is that they are dynamic. This means hot links can be embedded in the text. Clicking on a link can take the reader instantly to a different place in the book for related information, without having to thumb through pages. Other links may lead to destinations on the Internet.

In a novel or collection of stories or poems, the only necessary links will occur in the front or back matter. You will certainly want to link your Web site, blog, and/or Facebook location. You will probably want to link your author's e-mail address and Twitter handle.

In a nonfiction book, on the other hand, internal and external links can add enormous value to the reader. By unselfishly pointing to other information sources (including books that compete with yours), you gain credibility. Readers will appreciate and remember the extra steps you took to help them. Reviewers will be impressed by your research in the subject area.

Most word processing and desktop publishing programs make it easy to attach a URL to a text word or phrase. Spend time charting useful links and take advantage of this important tool.

Will the Book Be Illustrated?

Most works of fiction contain no illustration, apart from the book cover. If you've written an informational or how-to book, you may want to include visual aids. These might include your own digital photographs or drawings. You may be able to find free photos, pictures, charts, and graphs online. Read the provider's terms before you download an image, though. Some clip art is free only for use in nonprofit publications.

Illustration is an area where e-book publishing differs significantly from print publishing. Graphic designers use desktop publishing programs to prepare books for printing. They see in advance exactly how each page will appear in print.

E-book publishing engines operate more simply. You may be disappointed in how your book turns out if you submit a complex design. Images may appear in odd places—or may not appear at all. Color art may display in black and white.

Automated online tools for e-book preparation have improved. Apps for previewing a book before launching it, for example, are much better than they were a few years ago. They more accurately show the author/publisher how it will appear on readers' screens.

File   Edit   View   Favorites   Tools   Help

   CATCHY COVERS AND TITLES

CATCHY COVERS AND TITLES

An e-book author with a creative flair can personally design an adequate cover. Templates can make the process very easy.

The cover design may not require artwork. If you believe it needs an illustration, you may be able to find appropriate clip art, free.

Your book title is extremely important. Professional authors usually have a "working title" in mind as they write the manuscript. A better title often comes to them by the end of the project.

You should search the Internet for identical and similar titles. Because millions of books have been published, duplicate titles are unavoidable. Make your title as distinctive and clever as you can. A creatively worded subtitle will give readers a further idea of what the book is about. Your title and subtitle are the book's permanent identity, so consider them very carefully.

Layout and Design

Layout is the placement of type and images on the book's pages. Design is the overall theme and appearance of the completed project. You should learn the technical submission requirements of the publishing platform(s) you plan to use. You need to know how to set paragraph spacing and headline sizes, and where images can and can't be placed.

A key part of the design is the typeface in which text will appear to the reader. Thousands of typefaces are available. The outlandish ones are useful for zany posters but not for e-book text.

Photographs and other art forms can enliven any book. E-book publishers must take special care viewing their visual elements before and after launching because different devices display e-books differently.

Standard typefaces are in two categories. Serif typefaces feature short, subtle lines (serifs) at the ends of strokes that form each alphabetic letter or number. Sans serif typefaces lack the distinctive stroke ends. Serif typefaces are more elegant and are used in many printed books. Sans serif typefaces are plainer. They make it easier to read text on a computer or mobile device screen.

Some e-publishing platforms limit your options to only a few standard choices. Others let you submit the e-book in any typeface you wish but convert it automatically to a common typeface. To avoid a surprise, you should choose a popular typeface. Times New Roman, New Century Schoolbook, and Bookman are common serif typefaces. Arial, Tahoma, and Verdana are typical sans serif alternatives.

An especially challenging task is creating a dynamic table of contents (TOC). Ideally, each chapter or section entry in the TOC will link to the actual page within the book. Methods of creating a dynamic TOC can be somewhat involved. Some e-book authors create simple, static table of contents pages, merely listing the chapter titles.

Many authors are not interested in the technical ins and outs of e-book preparation. Numerous online

Many students have no interest in writing an e-book but are wizards at onscreen graphic assembly. They can be of great help in designing and launching your book project.

services offer to perform—for a fee—every task from editing and design to marketing. If you have no budget, you may have tech-savvy friends willing to handle the assembly and launching for you.

TEN GREAT QUESTIONS

TO ASK AN INFORMATION SPECIALIST

1 Should I register a copyright before I let anyone edit, proofread, or review my book?

2 What can I do if I discover someone has copied long sections of my book or is selling copies of my book online?

3 What can I do if a movie, song, or another book comes out with the same title as my book?

4 Which online distribution platform is best?

5 Will the distributor protect my work from being stolen or plagiarized?

6 If I sell a copy of my e-book as a PDF file, what's to prevent the buyer from sharing or even reselling it?

7 Why does my book appear differently on the screens of different reading devices? How can I make it look the same everywhere?

8 I'm now selling my e-book through an online distributor. How can I make free copies of it available to friends and relatives?

9 At what point should I consider looking for a marketing service or agent?

10 To take advantage of new e-publishing technology in the future, will I have to un-publish, reformat, and re-launch my book?

Chapter 3

Launching the E-Book

E-book publishing is based on the POD system of distribution. "POD" stands for "print on demand" or "publish on demand."

In print publishing, a publisher can print as few as one copy of a book. It would cost almost as much to produce that single copy, though, as it would to produce a thousand copies. Much time and money are invested in the preparation (prepping) process. After that work is done, the costs of paper and ink are the only significant expenses left in printing the book.

An e-book needs no paper or ink. Once it has been prepped, the finished project becomes an electronic file. The file can be sold "on demand" over the Internet to one customer or a million. Copies of the book are not actually distributed electronically until customers place orders for them.

E-Book Technology and Services

Numerous online services are available to prepare authors' books for them. Some can help produce both print and electronic books, as well as recordings and other products. Typically, they charge fees for various steps of preparation. If the author can perform all of the preparation, including cover design, there may be no fees up front, but there will be distribution costs.

Many e-book authors prefer to use the publishing and distribution platform of one of the established book distributors. Amazon, for example, offers a system for producing e-books that can be displayed on its Kindle devices. Barnes & Noble provides a similar system for its Nook e-reader format. The use of these systems for publishing, distribution, and sales processing costs the author nothing. However, the author is responsible for submitting the product acceptably, including the cover, front matter, and properly formatted text. The author must also promote the book, if it is to be successful.

Best-selling e-book author Amanda Hocking launched her first book for the Kindle audience. According to Pilkington, she also used the Smashwords service to make her book available for Nook, iBook, and Sony Reader devices.

"Online bookstores" such as Google eBooks provide convenient sales and distribution channels for e-book publishers. Some authors/publishers use more than one publishing platform and distribution system.

A key factor to consider is which platform will get your book the greatest exposure. You may decide to publish in one popular format (Amazon, Barnes & Noble, etc.) and focus your marketing plan on that platform. Many authors launch their e-books for multiple reader formats at once.

The Importance of Keywords

When launching your e-book, you will be asked to provide keywords you want to attach. Keywords draw interested readers to the book's online URL.

For a book about ocean diving, keywords might include "SCUBA," "snorkeling," "diving gear," "wreck diving," "coral reef," and "underwater life." For a biography of Wolfgang Amadeus Mozart, logical keywords would include "famous composer," "classical music," "child prodigy," and "Vienna." You also could list musical terms such as "piano," "violin," "sonata," "symphony," and "string quartet."

If you write fiction and your novel is a spy thriller, useful keywords may be "espionage," "CIA," "code," "false identity," "disguise," and "double agent."

File   Edit   View   Favorites   Tools   Help

INSTANT PUBLICATION METHODS

INSTANT PUBLICATION METHODS

Two simple formats for self-publishing your book are PDF and HTML. Many popular word processing and desktop publishing programs let you save files in PDF format. You can create a simple title display page and a page of basic front matter—copyright notice, author and/or publisher name, contact information, and table of contents. Your saved PDF file becomes an e-book. You can send the file as an e-mail attachment to whoever requests it.

Just as easily, you can paste the book text into a Web page creation program. Publish the page at your Web site in HTML format. The Web page becomes an online book. Readers can view it directly on the Internet.

Consultants advise marketers to be creative and thorough in developing keyword lists. E-book authors should give this step serious time. You should put yourself in the places of different readers who might be interested in your subject. It is smart to list as many appropriate keywords as you can think of—although some systems have keyword limits. Corey Perlman, author of *eBOOT CAMP*, suggests a range of fifteen to twenty-five keywords.

Pre-Launch Decisions

Before making your book public, you must decide several publishing issues.

Do you need to copyright the work in advance?

A copyright literally is an author's "right to copy" a work. That may seem meaningless, but it is all important. Whoever owns the legal right to copy a work controls the *sale* of copies. In short, the copyright holder owns the work. Thus, you need to establish your copyright.

Under common law, your book is copyrighted for you the moment you make the first copy of it. However, to ensure future legal protection, you must register your copyright with the Library of Congress. You can register a copyright claim online for as little as $35. To learn how, visit these Library of Congress sections online: http://www.copyright.gov and http://www.copyright.gov/forms.

Regardless of your copyright registration status, you should definitely indicate your copyright date in the front matter of the book. You can simply state "Copyright 2013 by [YOUR NAME]" or use the copyright symbol: "© 2013 by [YOUR NAME]."

Do you need an ISBN?

ISBN stands for "International Standard Book Number." This number identifies a specific book. Library book catalog information is tied to books'

Many e-book authors and publishers don't go to the trouble of registering copyrights with the Library of Congress or obtaining ISBNs for their books. In the long run, those omissions may be risky.

ISBNs. Bookstores that sell printed books require their ISBNs. If you expect to sell the book in print in the future, it may be wise to obtain the number now.

In the United States, the ISBN assigning agency is R.R. Bowker LLC. Bowker charges $125 to issue the ISBN for one book. For $250, you can obtain ten ISBNs; for $575, you can buy a hundred numbers—more than enough for all the books you probably will ever write. For details, go to http://www.isbn.org.

How will you get paid?

If you want to sell your book, you need to have a system in place to handle and fulfill orders (distribute the book) and process payments. E-book distribution platforms such as Amazon and Barnes & Noble make it simple. After you prepare your book according to their guidelines and launch it, the service provider does everything for you. The service makes the book available to online shoppers. It receives payment for orders and delivers the book online to purchasers. After deducting its percentage of profits, the service provider pays you your share. Some services pay monthly, others less frequently. Payments are almost always made electronically. Your money is deposited into your PayPal or bank account.

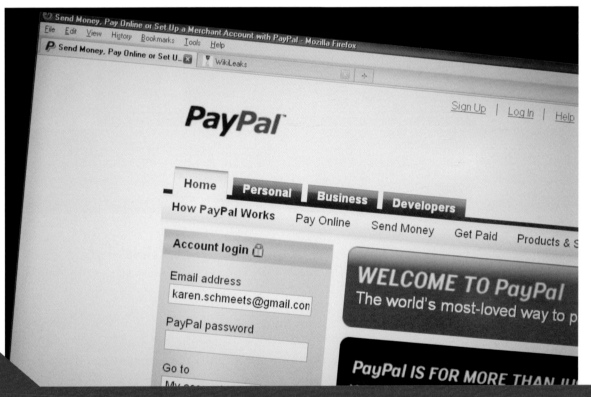

Payments to e-book publishers and authors are usually made by direct deposit into bank accounts or through PayPal, an intermediary buy-sell service.

If you self-publish the book as a PDF file, you can easily fulfill orders yourself. Simply send the book file to buyers via e-mail, or make it available for them to download from your Web site. To get paid for it, the old-fashioned way is to direct buyers to mail you a check. (Expect very few sales using this process.) You'll attract more customers if they can pay you online.

Typically, payment is arranged through PayPal. A person eighteen or older can set up a free PayPal account to make and receive payments online. PayPal offers advanced services for merchants (sellers) for a fee. Parents can create student PayPal accounts for their children.

Fee-based online selling services are available, such as E-junkie.

The convenience of order fulfillment and payment processing is a major reason why many authors publish their books through online distribution services.

Chapter 4

Finding a Readership

Many beginning authors offer their e-books free, at least for a while. They may be humiliated when, after weeks and months, little interest is shown in what they've written. Some writers, it seems, can't even give their books away.

Bad writing may not be the reason. An equally common problem is that writers fail to market their books effectively. Like any other marketable product, an e-book will not sell if no one knows it exists.

Some publishing professionals will tell you that if you want to be a successful book author, marketing is half the work. Others will tell you marketing is 95 percent of the work. Many full-time authors spend more time promoting their books—at book signings, lectures, and online—than they do writing them.

Marketing on the Internet

What makes e-book publishing work is the Internet. Naturally, then, the Internet is the primary place to publicize e-books. Cresta Norris, in her book

Blog, Podcast, Google, Sell, points out that online marketing "is not about word of mouth, but about search engine appeal."

If you have a Web site or blog, you can use it to spread the word about your book. You might post occasional excerpts from it. You can announce promotional events. As a service to your readers, you can provide links to Web resources that provide additional information about your topic.

If you don't have an author's Web site, you should create one. An author's blog can serve a similar purpose. Web users have come to expect blogs to be dynamic—updated regularly with new comments and ideas. Do not start a blog unless you are committed to keeping it fresh.

Meanwhile, you can use social networks such as Facebook and Twitter to keep up a steady chatter about your book. (Be aware of network service policies and tools related to promotional content.)

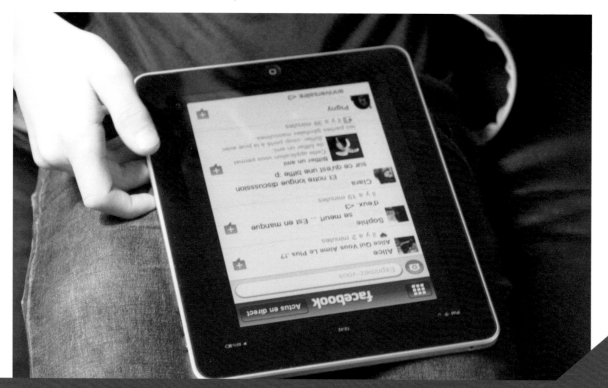

Millions of teenagers use tablet devices to network throughout the day—and to read books and periodicals. Naturally, social networking provides an excellent way to promote your e-book.

A customer (reader) contact database will be a tremendous aid for promoting future books. Before even launching your first e-book, you should begin building this computerized database. It will contain records of individuals who buy your book or who might want to buy it. You can maintain the list as an alphabetized word processing file. A contact program gives you greater options for managing your records.

Some contact databases simply keep customers' names and e-mail addresses. Some add information that can help conduct targeted promotional campaigns. Data may include a reader's special interests, how the reader found out about you, or the person's e-reading device type.

A podcast is a video or audio file you produce, record, and link to your Web site or blog. People who tune in can hear you discussing your book in person. You might involve other participants to discuss the book with you. Offer the podcast free of charge. However, use a simple registration form to obtain at least the name and e-mail address of each visitor. Add these contacts to your reader database.

Don't overlook simple marketing devices to promote your book. For example, every e-mail memo you send should conclude with a signature block identifying you as an author. The block should contain the title of your e-book and links to the book page and to your author's Web site or blog.

"Give Away My Book? You Must Be Kidding!"

An aspiring mystery writer launched six e-books through the Amazon Kindle platform. After a year averaging only two or three sales per month, the writer enrolled three of the books in Amazon's KDP Select program. This allowed Amazon Prime members to "borrow" the enrolled books, like checking them out of a library.

In a promotional experiment, the writer offered those three books free for five days. The results were astonishing. More than seven hundred customers in four countries "purchased" the three books during that period.

- □ X

File   Edit   View   Favorites   Tools   Help

   OFFLINE MARKETING IDEAS

OFFLINE MARKETING IDEAS

Marketing is vital for e-book publishing success. Leave no stone unturned in exploring marketing ideas. Here are a few examples.

Have T-shirts printed in bulk. Wear yours often. Give them to friends to wear. A picture of the e-book is enlarged on the back of the shirt. Hopefully, your author's Web site or blog has a short, simple address, and you can print that beneath the title. By simply roaming at a mall, concert, or sports event, you can publicize your e-book.

Design and print catchy posters containing information about your book and its Web link. Post them everywhere in town you're allowed to post. Print copies of informational cards and leave them in waiting rooms, bus stops, fast-food restaurants, etc.

Offer yourself as a public speaker. You can make presentations about the subject of your book, or about the toils and joys of becoming an e-book author. You might be invited to speak at library programs, civic meetings, and church events. Teachers may want you to talk to classes in your own school.

Write a press release to send to newspapers and broadcast media. (Most releases today are distributed by e-mail. Because of that, a release sent by postal letter may have a better chance of getting an editor's attention.)

With this newfound audience, the writer realized several benefits. The free books drew some of the readers to the author's other books, which began to sell. The author also observed an up-tick in Web site visits.

Making your book available (temporarily) for free is not at all foolish. A similar strategy is to prepare and publish a short e-book with no price. Its purpose is to attract readers and point them to your for-profit works.

Reviews Help Establish Your Book

A review of your e-book is an important form of free publicity. If you can obtain an objective pre-review—perhaps from a local newspaper book columnist or a literature teacher—it can be very useful. A pre-viewer might even be willing to write a personal introduction for your book.

Hopefully, some of your readers will take time to post reviews online. The more positive reviews, the higher a book will rank among the returns of keyword searches on the Web. You can include excerpts from reviews in your press announcements.

Caution: Don't falsify reviews, writing them yourself under assumed names. Also, don't solicit your friends or family members to post complimentary comments. Exposure of these tactics could hurt your reputation.

"Buying" a Readership

An e-book marketer needs a good understanding of how Internet search engines work. An effective keyword list is only one tool for generating search returns. Search engines automatically evaluate the content of a Web page in ranking its potential value to searchers. They sift through meta tags planted in the source code of Web pages.

The effective use of search engines has become a science in online marketing. Most young e-book publishers don't delve deeper than crafting their keyword lists. They simply make their books available and hope the search engines will bring satisfactory traffic to their book pages.

Those who can afford to invest money to improve sales might consider buying sponsored (pay-per-click) advertisements. Basically, you contract with a search engine company to include an ad for your book's URL among the

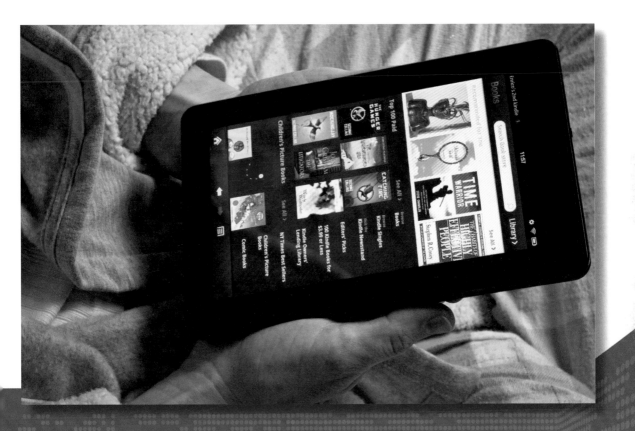

Users of tablet computers and e-reader devices have countless books, games, and other online resources available at the touch of the screen. Getting attention for your e-book is a challenge.

sponsored links that are displayed prominently in search result screens. You pay for each time a searcher clicks your link. The cost per click varies. A click could cost a dollar or more—and there's no guarantee any visitor to your book page will buy the book. For this type of marketing, it's smart to engage a professional who knows how to obtain the best return on your pay-per-click investment.

Hundreds of search engines are available to people browsing the Internet. Google by far is the most frequently used. Other leading engines include Yahoo!, Microsoft's Bing, and AOL.

Legal Concerns and Pitfalls

Besides paperwork such as copyrights and ISBN registrations, publishers have to deal with several legal concerns. These have to do mainly with securing the author and publisher's rights and ensuring that the book does not violate the rights of others.

The Author's Responsibilities

Essentially, your responsibilities as an e-book author and publisher are the same as those that have governed the printed book industry for many years. Media lawyers stress three basic precautions.

First, the material must be original. Stealing another's writing is called plagiarism. You can borrow other writers' ideas as long as you express them in your own words. To a very limited extent, you can include passages in your book that were written by other authors. You must enclose those passages in quotations and give credit to the sources. Writers for many years have done this, claiming the right of "fair use." How much quoted text you may use—and whether you may use it at all—depends. Court decisions have varied. In general, if your use of the material will benefit the source, you are probably safe. If the source could find it insulting, beware. The source would also be alarmed if you borrowed too much text. The U.S. Copyright Office advises writers to obtain permission from the source in advance.

The second danger is publishing unlawful criticism and insults. Americans enjoy freedom to criticize, but there are limits. False or overly cruel attacks on someone's reputation can get you in trouble. Lies and stabbing insults intended to injure a person's reputation are known as libel. (Slander is the act of deliberately injuring a person's character with spoken statements.) Jessica Dunn and Danielle Dunn, in their book *A Teen's Guide to Getting Published*, urge young writers to "think before you publish something you may regret later."

The third concern applies mainly to writers of nonfiction books: accuracy and thoroughness. Suppose you love to cook and you're publishing a small e-volume on your favorite ingredient, mushrooms. You discuss the nutritional value of certain wild mushrooms—but one of your illustrations misidentifies a poisonous species as nonpoisonous.

Or you're publishing an e-book about performing as a garage band. Your section on setting the stage provides excellent suggestions for novice roadies. But it fails

In legal terms, a published book is the author's and /or publisher's intellectual property. You should take steps to protect it. You must also avoid stealing or misusing the intellectual property of other writers.

Abigail Gibbs initially published her vampire novel on the Internet. It became so popular that a major publishing house signed her— at age eighteen—to a valuable contract to write two novels for print publication.

to caution them to secure offstage cables flat on the floor. At a performance, a dancer might trip and suffer a serious injury.

If your e-book becomes profitable, you have a legal responsibility of a different nature: taxes. Whether you sell your e-book file yourself or use an online e-publishing service, you must pay income taxes if you earn more than $600 a year. A tax preparer, accountant, or lawyer can tell you how to report income to the government and pay taxes.

Selling to an Established Publisher

It is difficult for teenage writers to find publishers for their work, beyond their school newspapers and yearbooks. In *A Teen's Guide to Getting Published*, the authors observe that it is especially hard for young book authors.

The explosive growth of e-book publishing has made it slightly easier for young authors to catch the attention of agents and editors at mainline publishing companies. Publishing executives are interested in sales potential. If an indie e-book sells ten thousand copies or more in its first year, a major

File   Edit   View   Favorites   Tools   Help

     BEWARE UNNECESSARY COSTS, EMPTY PROMISES, AND VAGUE TERMS

BEWARE UNNECESSARY COSTS, EMPTY PROMISES, AND VAGUE TERMS

Young writers who need to use an e-book preparation service should investigate the company's reputation. Some companies provide useful services well worth the fees. Others offer "services" that are costly and worthless to the author.

A student author might pay for editing and proofreading, for example. Afterward, the student may realize an English teacher or school newspaper editor could have done a better job.

Questionable marketing offers are rampant. A publishing or distribution service may drop hints that a manuscript is of especially high quality. For a substantial fee, the company guarantees global promotion. Of course, there is no guarantee of actual book sales. Years later, the author may have realized zero sales from the marketing scheme.

What will be the author's percentage (royalty) on each e-book sale? Is the author free to end the agreement at any time and self-publish the book, or contract with another publisher? If you sign a contract with an e-publishing company, what specific rights will the publisher control? For how long?

publisher might consider it.

At that point, the e-book author/publisher will need the advice of a literary agent and a lawyer. Issues to be agreed may include reprint rights, royalty percentages, and film rights. Contract details affect the division of profits, control of the book's contents, control of future publication, and rights involving future works by the author.

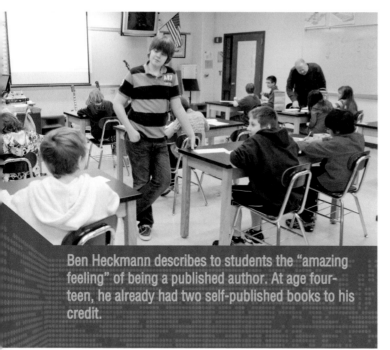

Ben Heckmann describes to students the "amazing feeling" of being a published author. At age fourteen, he already had two self-published books to his credit.

The E-Book Outlook

The e-book phenomenon provides a wide-open avenue for writers of any age to become published. How will it change in coming years? How will it impact the print publishing industry? Writers, publishers, online distributors, librarians, and the reading public all are interested to find out.

Critics are alarmed that the book market is becoming flooded with low-quality sludge. A Web search on any topic can lead to countless e-books of little informational or literary value. Anyone can publish a book preaching a viewpoint. Anyone can do a little research, publish an e-book, and thus claim to be an expert on the topic. Anyone can release a short, boring, sloppily written romance saga and take credit as a "novelist."

Consumers find it increasingly difficult to sort the good from the bad. Online booksellers try to provide guidance in the form of reader reviews —but many reviews are biased, written by friends (or enemies) of the writers. It remains to be seen whether a meaningful system for guiding e-book consumers will emerge.

Young authors must understand they face an awesome mass of market competition. Even if your work is excellent, you may be disappointed. The best-marketed e-books, including many of inferior quality, are most likely to sell.

But keep in mind your purpose as a writer. If your book provides the reading public with useful information or an interesting, well-written tale, you are a successful author.

copyright Author's or publisher's legal ownership of a written work; literally, the "right to copy" the work.

database Collection of information stored on computer.

genre Category of writing, music, or art, such as gothic, romance, or science fiction.

keyword Word or short term an online searcher types in order to find Web resources about a specific subject.

meta tag Word or phrase invisibly attached to an Internet page, intended to attract search engines to the page.

plagiarism Act of stealing someone else's writing.

royalty Author's share of profit from the sale of a book.

serif, sans serif Two general classes of typefaces; serif typefaces feature small lines (serifs) at the ends of character strokes, while sans serif character strokes are without the distinctive lines.

source code Programming language used to create a Web page.

template Design file that serves as a pattern, as for a book cover; it can be reused by different publishers who simply insert their own information in fields for the book's title, subtitle, byline, and art.

typeface Visual style of a printed character set.

URL Universal resource locator; the Internet address of a Web site, blog, book page, and so forth.

vanity printer/publisher A printing company that will print copies of a book for any author, for a fee.

FOR MORE INFORMATION

The Authors Guild
31 East 32nd Street, 7th Floor
New York, NY 10016
(212) 563-5904
Web site: http://www.authorsguild.org
The guild advocates copyright protection, fair contracts, and free expression
    for authors.

Bowker
630 Central Avenue
New Providence, NJ 07974
(888) 269-5372
Web site: http://www.bowker.com
The official ISBN agency for the United States, Bowker provides a book
    organizational and management system for publishers, bookstores, and
    libraries.

Creative Commons
444 Castro Street, Suite 900
Mountain View, CA 94041
(650) 294-4732
Web site: http://creativecommons.org
This nonprofit organization helps writers and other creative individuals share
    their work online, while setting conditions for shared use.

Independent Book Publishers Association
1020 Manhattan Beach Boulevard, Suite 204
Manhattan Beach, CA 90266
(310) 546-1818

Web site: http://www.ibpa-online.org
The Independent Book Publishers Association provides support, guidance,
    advocacy, and education for self-, small press, and independent
    publishers.

International Digital Publishing Forum
93 South Jackson Street, Suite 70719
Seattle, WA 98104
(206) 451-7250
Web site: http://idpf.org
This forum maintains the EPUB digital book format and "fosters enhanced
    communication between all stakeholders in the emerging global digital
    publishing industry."

Library of Congress
101 Independence Avenue SE
Washington, DC 20540
(202) 707-5000
Web site: http://www.loc.gov
The world's largest library provides, among many other services, information
    and forms concerning book copyrights.

Publishers Weekly
71 West 23 Street, #1608
New York, NY 10010
(212) 377-5500
Web site: http://www.publishersweekly.com
The industry standard periodical now includes sections of news and informa-
    tion about self-publishing and digital publishing.

Teen Ink
Box 30
Newton, MA 02461
(617) 964-6800
Web site: http://www.teenink.com
Teen Ink offers a magazine, book series, and Web site devoted to writing
and other creative art forms by individuals age thirteen through
nineteen.

Writer's Digest
F+W Media, Inc.
10151 Carver Road, Suite #200
Blue Ash, OH 45242
(513) 531-2690
Web site: http://www.writersdigest.com
Writer's Digest magazine is a longtime resource for aspiring and professional writers. The organization develops various writing and marketing
publications and online services for writers.

Web Sites

Due to the changing nature of Internet links, Rosen Publishing has developed
an online list of Web sites related to the subject of this book. This site is
updated regularly. Please use this link to access the list:

http://www.rosenlinks.com/DIL/eBook

FOR FURTHER READING

Dunn, Jessica, and Danielle Dunn. *A Teen's Guide to Getting Published*. 2nd ed. Waco, TX: Prufrock Press, Inc., 2006.

Fletcher, Ralph. *How Writers Work: Finding a Process That Works for You*. New York, NY: HarperCollins, 2000.

Fletcher, Ralph. *Live Writing: Breathing Life into Your Words*. New York, NY: HarperCollins, 1999.

"40 of the Best Web Sites for Young Writers." Education Portal, June 2011. Retrieved November 2012 (http://education-portal.com/articles/40_of_the_Best_Websites_for_Young_Writers.html).

Hanley, Victoria. *Seize the Story: A Handbook for Teens Who Like to Write*. Waco, TX: Prufrock Press, Inc., 2011.

Jakubiak, David J. *A Smart Kid's Guide to Internet Privacy*. New York, NY: Rosen Publishing, 2010.

Kalmbach, Mike. *Writing Advice for Teens: Creating Stories*. Scotts Valley, CA: CreateSpace, 2012.

Kamberg, Mary-Lane. *The I Love to Write Book—Ideas & Tips for Young Writers*. Milwaukee, WI: Crickhollow Books, 2008.

Levine, Gail Carson. *Writing Magic: Creating Stories That Fly*. New York, NY: HarperCollins, 2006.

Potter, Ellen, and Anne Mazer. *Spilling Ink: A Young Writer's Handbook*. New York, NY: Square Fish, 2010.

Selfridge, Benjamin, Peter Selfridge, and Jennifer Osburn. *A Teen's Guide to Creating Web Pages and Blogs*. Waco, TX: Prufrock Press, Inc., 2009.

BIBLIOGRAPHY

Becker, Michael, and John Arnold. *Mobile Marketing for Dummies*. Hoboken, NJ: Wiley Publishing, Inc., 2010.

Bosman, Julie. "Survey Shows Growing Strength of E-Books." *New York Times*, July 18, 2012. Retrieved August 2012 (http://mediadecoder .blogs.nytimes.com/2012/07/18/survey-shows-growing -strength-of-e-books).

Clarke, Michael. "Why E-Book Distribution Is Completely and Utterly Broken (and How to Fix It)." *Scholarly Kitchen*, November 2, 2012. Retrieved November 2012 (http://scholarlykitchen.org/2012/11/02 /why-e-book-distribution-is-completely-and-utterly-broken-and-how-to-fix-it).

Dunn, Jessica, and Danielle Dunn. *A Teen's Guide to Getting Published*. 2nd ed. Waco, TX: Prufrock Press, Inc., 2006.

Fahle, Rich. "Simon & Schuster CEO Carolyn Reidy: Everyone Needs to Think Digital" (with video). *Digital Book World*, July 9, 2012. Retrieved November 2012 (http://www.digitalbookworld.com/2012 /simon-schuster-ceo-carolyn-reidy-everyone-needs-to-think-digital-video).

Finder, Alan. "The Joys and Hazards of Self-Publishing on the Web." *New York Times*, August 15, 2012. Retrieved August 2012 (http://www. nytimes.com/2012/08/16/technology/personaltech/ins-and -outs-of-publishing-your-book-via-the-web.html?_r=3&ref=todayspaper&).

Flood, Alison. "Stop the Press: Half of Self-Published Authors Earn Less Than $500." *Guardian*, May 24, 2012. Retrieved December 2012 (www.guardian.co.uk/books/2012/may/24/self-published-author -earnings?intcmp=239).

Gootman, Elissa. "Young Writers Dazzle Publisher (Mom and Dad)." *New York Times*, March 31, 2012. Retrieved November 2012 (http:// www.nytimes.com/2012/04/01/us/young-writers-find-a -devoted-publisher-thanks-mom-and-dad.html).

Herman, Jeff. *Jeff Herman's Guide to Book Publishers, Editors, and Literary Agents 2012*. Naperville, IN: Sourcebooks, Inc., 2011.

Macy, Beverly, and Teri Thompson. *The Power of Real-Time Social Media Marketing*. New York, NY: McGraw-Hill, 2011.

Miller, Michael. *The Ultimate Web Marketing Guide*. Indianapolis, IN: Que Publishing, 2011.

Norris, Cresta. *Blog, Podcast, Google, Sell: The Complete Guide to Making Online Profit*. Philadelphia, PA: Kogan Page Limited, 2012.

Perlman, Corey. *eBOOT CAMP: Proven Internet Marketing Techniques to Grow Your Business*. Hoboken, NJ: John Wiley & Sons, Inc., 2009.

Pilkington, Ed. "Amanda Hocking: The Writer Who Made Millions by Self-Publishing Online." *Guardian*, January 12, 2012. Retrieved December 2012 (http://www.guardian.co.uk/books/2012/jan/12/amanda -hocking-self-publishing).

Poynter, Dan. *Dan Poynter's Self-Publishing Manual, Vol. 2*. Santa Barbara, CA: Para Publishing, 2009.

INDEX

A

Amazon, 22, 23, 26, 30
AOL, 33
apps, 16

B

back matter, 16
Barnes & Noble, 22, 23, 26
Bing, 33
blogs, 16, 29, 31
book publishing, future of, 11–12
book titles, 17
Bowker, 25

C

contact databases, 30
copyright, 20, 23, 24, 34, 35
cover design, 16, 17
credibility, gaining, 11, 16

D

desktop publishing programs, 16, 23
Dunn, Danielle, 35
Dunn, Jessica, 35

E

e-book, publishing your,
    assembling it, 14–19
    finding readers, 28–33
    launching it, 21–27
    legal aspects, 24, 34–38
    myths and facts, 13
    overview, 4–12
eBOOT CAMP, 24
E-junkie, 27

F

Facebook, 16, 29
fair use, 34
film rights, 37
front matter, 16, 22, 23, 24

G

Google, 33

H

Heckmann, Ben, 9
Hocking, Amanda, 7–8, 22
HTML, 23

I

iBook, 22
illustrations, 16, 17, 35
information specialist, ten great questions to
    ask an, 20
ISBNs, 24–25, 34

K

keywords, 13, 23–24, 32
KidPub Press, 9
Kindle, 22, 30

L

libel, 35
Library of Congress, 24
literary agents, 4, 13, 20, 37

M

meta tags, 32
Microsoft, 33

N

Nook, 22
Norris, Cresta, 28–29

O

offline marketing ideas, 31
order fulfillment, 26–27

P

PayPal, 26, 27
pay-per-click ads, 32–33
PDF files, 20, 23, 27
Perlman, Corey, 24
plagiarism, 20, 34
podcasts, 29, 30
Poynter, Dan, 9
print on demand (POD), 21
Project Gutenberg, 6
proofreading, 14, 15, 20, 37

R

reader databases, 30

reprint rights, 37

reviews, 16, 20, 32, 38
royalties, 37

S

Self-Publishing Manual, Vol. 2, 9–10
slander, 35
Smashwords, 22
Sony Reader, 22
source codes, 32
subtitles, 17

T

table of contents (TOC), 19, 23
taxes, 36
Teen's Guide to Getting Published, A, 35, 36
Twitter, 16, 29
typefaces, 17–19

U

U.S. Copyright Office, 35

V

vanity printing companies, 6

W

word processing programs, 14, 16, 23
working titles, 17

Y

Yahoo!, 33

About the Author

Daniel E. Harmon has written more than eighty print books, mainly educational works for young readers. His eight published e-books include seven collections of historical mystery short stories and a history of the *Titanic* disaster, *On a Sea So Cold and Still*. He is a longtime periodicals editor and the author of thousands of newspaper, magazine, and newsletter articles.

Photo Credits

Cover and p. 1 (left, right) Hannelore Foerster/Getty Images; cover and p. 1 (middle left) lev dolgachov/Shutterstock.com; cover and pp. 1 (middle right), 35 iStockphoto/Thinkstock; p. 5 EyesWideOpen/Getty Images; p. 8 David Brewster/MCT /Landov; p. 10 Bloomberg/Getty Images; p. 11 Emmanuel Dunaud/AFP/Getty Images; p. 15 Gary S. Chapman /Photographer's Choice/Getty Images; p 18 PRNewsfoto/AP Images; p. 19 Ghislain & Marie David de Lossy/Stone/Getty Images; p. 22 Justin Sullivan/Getty Images; p. 26 Karen Bleier/AFP/Getty Images; p. 29 Till Jacket/Photononstop/Getty Images; p. 33 iStockphoto.com/Bosca78; p. 36 Rex Features via AP Images; p. 38 Sara Jorde/The New York Times /Redux; cover (background) and interior page graphics © iStockphoto .com/suprun.

Designer: Brian Garvey; Editor: Kathy Kuhtz Campbell;
Photo Researcher: Amy Feinberg